vein

collected *poetry by*

ALLISON MARIE CONWAY

GLORY BEGIN PUBLISHING

Printed in the United States of America
First Printing, 2016

ISBN: 978-0-9977234-0-3

Glory Begin Publishing
www.glorybegin.com

for my mom.
for all the things she got to say
and all the things she didn't.

table *of* contents

introduction

I know exactly when a poem is about to pour through.

There is a splitting moment just before it comes that is the most pleasurable frustration.

It's a ripping surge and an ecstatic tug at the veins. Something physically moves the words into being.

I believe that at some level all artists are physically in tune not only with their work but also with the inspiration that comes before they begin the work.

Before we even pick up a pen or a paintbrush or a camera, we are touched by something.

We are sensationally alerted to the inspirational messages and in some strange way we are guided, prodded, coaxed, tempted, seduced, fingered, stroked, shocked, shoved, and caressed into birthing our mystical creations.

Something outside of us reaches in and decides to do whatever it takes to grab us.

I wrote this collection of poems because I am completely bewitched by this mysterious flow of energy that moves through my body whenever I have the privilege of writing something that begs to be written.

I can't tell you what that energy is as sure as I can't tell you what put the blood in my veins but I do promise you this: I can feel it.

I promise you it exists.

And I believe it reaches for all of us in the hopes that we will reach back. We want to touch each other in the most beautiful, intimate, and loving of ways. It is affection, it is reverence, it is selfless, it is real.

Vein is a tribute to that electric, pulsing energy that connects us more deeply to our humanity, our divinity, ourselves and one another. This creative life force moved through me in order to touch someone else.

That someone is you.

I thank you for holding this book in your hands. In this moment we have been connected by something bigger than ourselves.

I cherish our magic.

I hope that as you read this poetry you will, too.

With all my deepest love and gratitude,

Allison Marie

vein

ALLISON MARIE
CONWAY

// smoke //

undressing and descending
a velvet spiral stack of
stairs (these aren't level and i know it but
they always
stake my hesitance on broken
heels)
you sit on the floor not quite waiting not quite
gone,
reading aloud from a wordless
text
and want to know
how the gravel in your voice
makes me feel?
hard, my thief,

like Cat's Eye marbles between your thumbs
sliding along my
jaw.
burdened,
like seven aching limbs fighting
to play a
broken guitar in a room with the keys
locked outside in a running car.
exposed,
like gigantic beating wings severed and held together
hanging by the ends
of catgut
strings.
but the quiet ones hold their breathing
sharp
as if the way i paint my eyes
black
could turn the crimson light
inside us
dim.
you think it's a game because
i've learned to time my steps
to the parting of your lips
to your fingers
to the gentle stroke
that
turns me over like dismissive
pages.
tongue me with a forked irreverence, i
promise
this will all be over before
the elevator to the
basement
snaps.
even the finest cages,
angel,
never think they'll
last.

// resurrection //

falling never felt so
much like
ghost hands grabbing for
the heat of throats
and i'm so completely
full
of all the words
we choke instead of
feed each other
on.
all the king's horses
and all the clever gods of men and you fell
apart yesterday eating
teeth from my
hands.
now i light
fires in the
morning and sing for the soak of rain
all afternoon.
bed the sun behind
the screens, spread my
fingers one
by one
watch my mouth as i count
the times you needed
nothing
else,
and i will raise you up
again.
this time, lover, when the dawn comes
i will let it
break us
both.

// push //

nothing coats the skin more like surrender
than the drench of thorough rain across the
languid miles. it seems to take forever to
reach my tongue no matter how
fast it
falls and i
bend too much like a field of headless
fickle stems.
bare
knees to the scratch of heels on the
pavement, your heavy fingers distort the
curve of my fumbling
advances but i
can't see through this
fog and i
can't speak through this
mouth full of
sin and i
like it
this way
for
now.

// carrion //

in case they don't find the
bones
know they were fragile and
they were meant to be.
they were the way griffins
fell fast in the wind
like arrogant clouds
thrown from the
maniacal
sky.
the way you make reckless love
in a dream
and vanish
before it's
done.
and even without a lion's eyes,
without a mouth to match the words,
without a single tie that binds,
tell the ones who don't believe,
that i caught
the brutish beasts
by their razor claws,
one by violent one,
just to
study
their
wings.

// manners //

drink me like
heavy smoke
eat me like a coaxing
deliberate fog
swallows the blackest thickest rolling
hills
as they wait for
nothing.
lay me out in a thousand gowns
made of tentacles,
chains,
feathers,
and save them all
for
later.

// trouble //

feed to me the shocks of heat that
snap along your bones in the dark
that my words may breathe
into
you
like fire.
lick relentless at the prize of your
prophetic disaster
as smoke sets
decades of fallen forests free to collapse in ravenous flames.
numb is all the rage but we
can't stop touching and
you don't want out of

this
do
you?
only the kind of rain that rips open
lockets with crow bars,
slits the caps off your aging secrets,
launches relief like cannons,
swings hard enough to pound steel gongs
out of
 the metal plates you cross like hatchets over your heart.
only the torrential wet cascade
slamming in catastrophic waves
along our crumbling sides
(the water softens everything, my love, but not between
your thighs)
could ever even dream
of swallowing
your sacred
savage
hunger
down
tonight.

// neophyte //

i would play
in the dirt and the
sand and the dark
and let the things i imagined
consume my little bones.
somehow being young and new at it
turned my breathing into stars,
made the pages taste like
necklace candy under blankets on the moon
in my yard,
and scribbled my
mixed up
awe struck
poems
like monster
kisses
softening
the
night.
i still
go home
in the haunt of the heat of the
summer
laced with gold bracelets, bubblegum
lip gloss and
wind chimes.

// ego //

what is this phantom
mirrored
 image you
scream inside
for?
what is this search you
 move your slick melodic body
against the painted walls
of your animal mind
for?
describe the lines (are they moving toward you or away? it will
matter but you won't know
why)
the image you see
these images of me
what, beloved,
before we roll it up like tired
playbills, the curtains behind your eyes close,
switch off the whirring projector, someone's singing
voice is severed to staccato rhythm by
the blades of
a fan.
face the pools of light and speak:
how would you like us
to flash the damage
in pornographic scenes
across
your private
gaping
screen?
no one's bought a ticket but
we ask that you thank them
all for
coming.

// wait //

what of the
madness of birds
what of the
punish of feathers
barely touching
skin
what of the way the words
spread like beads
bruises scissors fangs
against
the flesh we amuse
ourselves in.
and all the detailed pages you
discard
melt like tissue
paper
taffy
bleeding
from my mouth
sentence after glistening sentence that took five hundred
years of calculated breeding
to
come
out.

// mausoleum //

i drink the rain
through my skin
like
alien limbs nobody
wants
anymore
this is the morning i
recall its coming
in (you feel it, too, i
can practically sing to it).
my nails in the dirt in
the ground are the push
reaching down.
a strangle of worms and
we've thickened
our imagined
collective writhing
loss - my god, these
metallic drops are heavy
for being
so thin
but you don't have to hold me
down
everything's a skull and its bride
and, little gravedigger, you
can't catch fast enough
what's
caving in.

// solicitous //

feminine magic
strokes the tall pink sloping
stems of this delicate
morning
into feathered mystic
twisted
repose.
the side of my face is
every side of the mountains all over
the world
reflected in your hands.
i'm the powder blue
of restless pleasured
peaceful bliss
not for
you
not with or without the length of
you
just me.
in this succulent melting
dawning haze, imagining the
taste
of the way a thousand porcelain
petals
fall
open
drowning of heat
inside of the
daze.

// film //

feed me what gnaws at you while it still
aches, i'd like to taste
the pain
let the marrow in the bones
of it draw crooked winged circle rings
around
your neck,
wrists,
ankles,
sex.
do what needs to be done for hours
laid end to end to end
pressing from the wet
of the dirt to the veins

in the
rocks inside
the sun
ripping the pleasure you administer apart
again, my sins
collapse against your feet.
rusted rails drag slits of dying into winter
cigarettes stain the forgotten streets
snow stings its naked legs into
spring and we all wait silent in our seats
in this abandoned lusty velvet
theater;
watch the breaks in the mindless bodies on
screen
as you collect your
things.

// slip //

the sweet collapse of every whetted thing
begins
on its own, lover,
you are not the first to buckle
and i'll not be the
last
thing on your shackled
mind
as the phantoms take their stabs but
miss
and the
ghosts reach out to stroke and disturb
you from
behind.
nails to the skin
rupture the thoughts they spin
the pain of the change rushes in;
ashes to ashes
we all crash down
but the ache in the break
makes the sharpest man
blind
and
 the flecks of blood on the petals you
feed me slide
off
just
fine.

// dirt //

i refuse to believe that exploring
the darkness
dims the light.
the eyes of love
are sharp enough to cut every limb
from every jagged tree
without flinching.
the ventricles of love
cannot close,
the mind of love cannot
deceive.
place your bloody hands to my
dirty mouth and tell
me why the screaming
stops.
paint my skin with your
bedtime stories,
build a staircase
with the swords they
threw at me.
and i will not bend
and i will not break
and i will not be threatened
by the things
they tell me
i can't
take.

// because //

i will take the menacing sunlight and turn it into
the softest rain
i know you like the
way it falls.
i will take the screaming and turn it into
the slightest steady breath
i know you like the way
that sounds.
and even as you twist your thorny
mind around such fears as being
left
being abandoned
being crucified lost banished mistreated
ridiculed threatened cheated
i will wait for you to let go
of them.
as long as it takes, time doesn't
matter the least bit to me
i have been waiting all this time and i will wait
out eternity to see
you fly
to hold your head up high
to live as though i live
for you and know at last,
beloved,
why.

// apocalypse //

heat from the sun slides along her back
and every bloodless object in the room
pressed against vases, doors wrenched at their hinges
mobs of quivering hands around a single
heart.
nowhere to go
nothing left to close
statues mask their eyes in long black shadows
looming covetous along the holes in the floors
and the disintegration of the day
buries the length of her face
in the mattress, face down.
some silences are only the memory of gestures
never made or ventured, some
we'd just as soon forget.
just as easy to fold our slender ravished bones
inside
the nests of giant ancient birds, clutched in their claws
as they fly quiet across an apocalyptic sky
i don't paint these pictures
or fantasize this destruction
but the gray in the dust collects as though
this was all the way
it was supposed to fall so desperately
so beautifully
apart
at the end of the end
of a
long
and oblivious
day.

// artist //

every star fell down at once
in the backlit thick this morning
slammed through the fog i wore
destroyed and delivered each other
before taking me, they won't leave.
i lay on them but cannot sleep
feed on them and try to scream
and all they ever offer me is fire
gutting through my bones
they'll tell you stars burn out
eventually
they don't know it's every single one
in me.

// speakeasy //

if they'd let me speak i'd tell you this:
they never said
this ink is not for drinking, child,
nor is the darkness yours.
so in my thirst i let
the poetry bite my lips
and in my nakedness
the words assembled
and bled me
for a kiss.

// eternity //

remember how this feels
hands in the dirt
knees on the pavement
face to the mouths in the sky
because you can't take it with you, beloved,
not the succulence in the catastrophe
not the torture in the ecstasy
read for me the wordless
breathe into me the codes
that suck at the sweat inside your wrists
taste capitulation as it comes
and remember,
remember, remember
this.

// breed //

if you could see through me
i would lose my mind.
lower your gaze and pull the rain down with your fists
heavy in constant punishing sheets
slide it down the inside of the walls
around and inside
me.
in the dark we remember the taste of our skin
the choke in the rush of the drowned out hours
was never meant to make us wet
but to baptize the ache and make offerings
of the animal seething within.

// ground //

i believe in the freedom of the empty
streets.
in the seconds before the time we've made up
changes, but not in the time
itself.
i have faith in grinding out the agony of my desires
in the sharp gravel
of my mind.
i believe in the
silence they feed me
and as they talk i listen.
i believe we walk alone as we walk beside

each other
as we need and receive and explore
each
other
and i believe we walk
a thousand miles for the mystery of pleasure
and of
pain
only to be reminded again
and again and again
that we're never as sure as we'd like to be
which shoes belong to whom
and that the only things we cling to
are the only things we
lose.

// kid //

quiet plugged the ears in the street
i noticed every window
every door
every iron and concrete
staircase, made notes in my
subconsciousness
memorized how the maps folded back and
forward
back and forward
a dozen times within a dozen times
withdrawing into themselves, collapsing all
the
world in leather, sliding up my sleeve.
the grates in the street are a design i was
taught
what they cage off, where they lead
i'm a kid on a bike in the wind in the sky
plotting the webs of my silence in the lids of my eyes.
they know my escape
and i know
where they
hide.

// break //

the bend in the mind is the adoration we
undress
hold my head still and listen for the crease
i can taste the dust in the clocks on the walls
collecting the dirt in our teeth
lies in the truth of every word
work me like knots through locks of hair
in padlocks chained around your neck
to remember i'm here or you're not alone -
which is it, servant or master or free?
snow can't help but sting the trees
i wait in a room upstairs and watch the fleshy pink
centers of geometry and religion
fall
on my knees for your needs
something in the room in the mind
behind the mind
opens every hand that ever closed
around mine
shadows marching as the time recedes
and the bend in the dark is the catch
and
release.

// hunger //

i swallow the hours whole like a wild child
starving
like beautiful destruction roaming pulling
veins from the wrist
searching the darkness for movement
night and day flash in the curve of my
wide nocturnal eyes, i can see the yellowed lights
on fire across the planet all of them too small
hopeful, quiet and alone.
my focus rips the shriveled earth in two and
offers it up to hang over the stars like snakes
writhing in the trees
they penetrate me in godly heat.
tell us anything: we'll believe
feed us what's left and we'll pretend
it's food
enough.

// celestial //

thick
fingers beg and trace the clamor
in her mind, she tries to hide.
thorough
fingers press down the breast
bone
a butterfly effect spreads glass wings on her
insides.
thirsty
fingers glide in circles unfastening the wrists
and all the sky's a
hedonistic turquoise night
soft tongues lapping at spearheads
stabbing licks at the edge of the threat of
release
five thousand years of fingers tear at a
world worn down, a galaxy runs out.
hold this to your stomach and sit.
all the shadows you spin are a
cataclysmic risk she needs.
but nature's fingers won't let up
they keep the pace
they rupture time
they tempt the words of the prophets
bled from her hands, stained on her lips
toxic drops of disarming digital codes
a covenant to make certain that the lives she
missed
keep her coming back ravaged and hungry
for nights
splayed out
like this.

// diastolic //

writing like this
in the way i've somehow
learned to do
with me sitting here
and you

being you
it's like between us we've grown a fragile
heart.
and if you listen
very closely
to the words and the craters
stepping on the moon
and look for shifting shapes in shadows
with the most beautiful eyes i've
never seen,
right now,
together,
we can watch it
beat.

// cheap //

just let the rain slide down
and wet
the
street
just let the dragons teach us
how to breathe
and in this world where the broken words
are going cheap
i'll close my mouth
and bed the rain
and let you take them
all
from
me.

// fractals //

move my desire inside the lines, inside the
lines
inside the outside of the lines i've peeled
underneath the pieces you struggle to see
when you
look
at me
staring at you behind the face
in the breaks in the glass
we reach out for the bend in the bend in the
eyes
for the visions sleeping within
stand close enough to fall apart
summon these vibrations
and kneel in them, swim.
penetrate the depths of the flames along the rim
my heat comes liquid, cascades in waves
streams of her energy plunging down
through
this
skin.
i fold my own hands, find my own thoughts
counting each finger: one
at
a
time, two, three, and then they fall off
to the side.
paint our eyes black to focus the mind but
when the lines that draw you
in place no longer collect the shape of your
face
it's hard to decide if it's
too
late.

// spine //

i don't want to tell you
how the darkness feels
hot like metal
poured inside my amenable spine
or the way
it turns the white noise
ripe.
i want to make you feel it
sliding off the bones
yourself.

// moonchild //

a single sleight, one trigger of a tortured nod
and the dregs of neglected solar systems come up
in your throat
like splintered wooden shipwrecks
below caverns in the ocean caving in
on the heads of the pricks of pins
held too tight against my skin,
the drag of a thousand alien arms stretched around
the galaxy that contains this world and all the worlds
between us.
as these threads through my fingers spin
thinning lines, retracted distractions
nestle again into places unassigned
but suggested. she always returns, collects the fractures
of flesh and puts them back
together in silence
like drops that surrender their shape
to lakes on the moons
inside her.

// soak //

radio static is coming in sharp now
an addictive prick of snapping and shussshhh
your voice is mourning or a
laugh, symbols of a language i was taught
but discarded.
i pull the shades and damp sheets
over me, press together my lashes,
my thighs,
my ear to this machine.
the noise makes everything in the room, in my mouth,
soak.
the rain is falling up into the stars, made to watch
our attempt at light competing
it's hollow but the transmitter picks it up
a ricochet of thoughts stampeding
the thunder of a thousand wings thrusting in my chest
every heart that ever tried and missed
still beating.

// pin //

even my dreams come to me in dreams
nothing is ever as hopeless as it seems
look again, take my hands and pin them
we don't need any further distraction
the night is strong and dark enough
i'm still as death but hot as flame and i know that's
hard to see, nothing this way makes sense.
drag your gaze along the cutting
of the lights, stabbing belief systems
clear through my eyes
where had you gone all this time?
if i lie down and you stand up
the things i remember remain the same
the breath breathes on its own
blood will always flow with its blood
and the heart beats only to clutch itself
even dreams have dreams, angel,
even wings grow wings.

// tonic //

and all along we could
taste the tonic of truth in the
roping of our fevered tongues
this life is feeding itself
into death,
death into life.
we never questioned after this
the seduction
the transfiguration
the crush or the rise of
the air through our
lungs.

// plead //

darkness quiets itself and slows my
breathing,
as i welcome centuries of ancient want
to collapse the ache beneath my skin.
my shoulders pull against the weight of time
but
hold the shape of her shape
and slender static of the
strong ones
who came before, we are grateful for
their pressing silence and
their
sage advance against what resistance we
had
left.
this is the pleasure and the burden we
accept.
streams of mad
release
paint themselves deep
in the bone that designs my face.
what will you see in her when these eyes
open, widen, search you?
be still and touch your hands
together.
the visions have begun their feeding of
her,
pull the veils and be patient.
we do not deliver time but allow it to deliver
us.
blades of a thousand knives and thieves,
wives and midwives
dance behind the seal of the closing of
contorted eyes

inside your mind. please,
reject what has been lost and listen
for the stretch of wings bending
strong into shadows wrenched between
sheets
the blood in our veins again begins its moving,
we pulse by memory on command
out over stones, gnawing steady at the walls
protecting what she
sees.
i watch.
souls breed skeletons, every synapse, every
cell remembers.
darkness only carves the light and
i am ready for what
comes.

// attention //

this is what it feels like to be watched -
had you missed the intrusion?
listen for the falling in the distance
muted by the blindfolds of a night
not yet broken, listen:
the buzzing of an old electric lamp
beside your head, tilted back against the wall;
it snaps and burns
out. (still watching?)
you can hear that, too, the burning
out of plugged together lights running ripped through
gutted floorboards
and the scattered pattern of the motion
of shifting gears in bodies in machines
the burning out of morning. listen
hard now, and again and again
for the burning out of the flesh of the days unpromised,
the burning out of
you.

// palm //

released from what it was that held me in two
wrist pulled from my wrist
side held to my (blind) side
head over my hands over my head
palm to my skin, your song is a scream and i bleed
every last thing is forbidden, look on this wall
it's all written down that you are to chant in the dark, whisper
down the hall where other people live, turn the lights
out it's all
over
now
and the rush feels fine
like a dozen waiting swords sheathed along my thighs
until you play the keys i can't dislodge from my chest
this searing haunt is so ecstatic
it collapses all the muscle we had left in
the heat
a page too sharp
a drop too steep
and a fight held fast
becomes too
weak.

// cage //

if these grim trees could
be so brash to claw their
crooked mess against
the punishing sky
why hold back
the fangs from the fences
why not swing your seven heads
of fire outside
the lines
and let the tears
and the screams
and the dust
and the beautiful raging
sadness
fly.

// fade //

forgive us our temptations, we
are but the way
our faceless shadows
fall against the steel frames
of mutilated buildings
in the fading of the concrete
sun
this evening.
for all our bargaining and pleading
there are flashes of light we refuse.
here comes the lust for the body,
here the truth begins receding.
i'm so sorry, my hungry distorted love,
i'm barely food enough
and with all the wires they've disconnected
there's little more
worth seeing.

// lies //

this is how your bones turn
to liquid heavy metal
and i drink.
this is how we turn the darkness
up
and the silence drops your defenses
down.
this is how we run
by night vision.
this is how we burn.
this is where we make up

for all the things they never
told us and this is why when every
star and every bridge and every knee
and every lie falls
they don't make
a
sound.

// black //

the window took the warmth of her mouth
her pain against the pane, suspended.
eyes reaching out for the heavy fog
as it swims across a frozen snowscape, receding.
sucking and spinning, the ice and the vapors
consume and release one another
like ghosts moving steady along in the dark
never coming up for air but
close.
black paints itself black; she submits
to the cold
blows every row of
candles out
one by one by one by one, then
undresses.
specters without eyes, without mouths, without faces,
and you
inside your pale perfect skin
crawl toward the daybreak blind and never look
back
in.

// recipe //

make the sound of who i am in the white noise
drag it all down and fill it with holes
in the ground.
i'm not waiting any longer for this.
rush along caverns of barbed wire
laced in vain.
i'm not where you thought i'd be.
fold yourself three times and let me watch.
open up: taste familiar? this is the recipe
we measured ourselves
for a thickened crush of dragon's heads
twisted like vines around the whirl of blades
in these elegant words.
i've gone and left everything so
what is this worth
the hand in my hand
is just your skeleton
distracted
with mine.

// currency //

melting,
the candy of you drips
its final drop into me
there will come a time when exposure
will be the only seductive and appreciated
currency.
an ancient debt will be required of you
to return
and willingly you'll give it
up.
until then, false gods watch the shadows
genuflect before crisscrossing the streets
alone
as you sit on the painted edge of a wooden chair
with pinned together legs, listless,
staring into the face
of a clock.

// jaw //

from up close it was stranger still:
the eyes seemed alive only enough to
rake themselves all
over you
over you slow.
and you, in this dim light, first refuse
then hesitate
then agree.
step back - we're halfway between
his desperate expression and
where to put
you.
what is this that covers your mouth, beloved?
where are the chains they used
to hinge the jaw to the heart
and would you like
us to see that you get
them back?

// afraid //

tell me this and i'll release
your hands, my love, be still:
how much do you
hold back?
how much do you blister to say
with lungs collapsing in.
how often do you bite that
truth lusted tongue and what
do you sell yourself for
blindfolded, wet with
a taste for things that collect the air
from those precious glossy veins
you carry on pulsing in
the dark
what are you afraid of
caving in
on you?

// skeletons //

please keep your voices down
we're about to start.
she's backstage and sick and
has already forgotten her lines.
what if they've memorized this scene
before
and when the lights roll up
her velvet cloak, and you
discard your drink and your mask and rip the playbills

down
there's nothing there to
critique?
"where do i begin if i don't buy a
single word." {lead strokes woman's cheek}
if the eyes in the heads can't see me
how can i be read? my god.
how we smile, bow down and butcher
the skeletons of things
we've not even
said.

// denial //

moonlight catches and follows itself
carving across tall trees at night and
i stare out, fighting sleep.
frozen flashes of white lace fingers
feeling up the legs of the street.
i shatter open to the cling of chimes
at the motionless hands of a stoic angel
as they rattle against the wind at your back
when you rush in
too late.
as i lie at your feet
the backlit menace behind the glass is
tracing another face across my face.
i could be anyone in silence.
you could be anyone before the sun rises.
we could be anyone but still
i deny
this.

// scream //

you can feel it when the seasons
click.
you can feel it when ice
breaks your fall and you bleed.
you can taste it in the cold air
between our mouths
as we walk all night
through the streets.
we are not here forever, we are not
wrapped in legs and arms and skin.
you can touch it but only in
frames,
hold it like a ghost down the hall
is a plaster face at your window.
time is a thief and a gift
and a scream.
you can feel it.

// centerfold //

these pages i could swear would
birth beating hearts just to
slash ink upon themselves
if i didn't
do it.
they would read your mind if
i didn't
and wrap around mattresses on fire.
they would shred centerfolds and
flick pin-ups into fishnet trash
cans swinging on poles
in parks in the city.
the words are all the same: thrown out,
used, misused, misled, misleading.
Forget The Words.
they would only unscrew the fingers from my body
like unwinding a clock
if i didn't pull them down from their towers
and watch.

// regret //

every hour was counted in decades
of plastic beads strung together
creeping along your fingers
like floorboards creaking into the scene
of our last stale morning alone
with time left.
this coffee and your blood is cold. creatures of the night
rewind by the wet of street lamps
and everything that made ecstatic sense before
replays like lunacy now.
those were the hours we held as they held us; that
hammered into place these floors
into these walls that watch us
breaking down
and we don't even question how.

// hands //

hand over hand crossed
behind my back
opening my mouth
on the ground
under my skin
across the world
in your closet
fingering electric wires
running through your veins
along my lips
against your naked
ear
to my chest
beating, pressing, holding,
stroking, touching
myself
to a mirror
reaching for
yours.

// triggers //

give me sunrise after throwing swords
and strong coffee at 2:22am. doing
odd things with you
at odd hours
so that if we were to leave
these mad days behind
or lay each other
aside for good

vein

i'd still have crooked triggers
of hours and things
done strangely
in ways
only we
understood.

// snow //

spread me fully open like
powder white sky: mute.
gray washed and oppressive enough
to crowd out the crush of steel beams,
calendars and clocks.
when the heat you need is ice pressed against my
neck, and the middle of the day - the middle of
you (against a body i've not met) - are holy
somber light, and as the sharpest bird in the
blackest dress clutches the highest stick
of a naked tree, even the shadows in this room
begin to come
like the sting of snow just before it falls
into the street,
into these sheets,
and into me.

// expectations //

we could have been anyone waking up across high rise
buildings from each other across the ocean, we could have
been: disfigured, dismembered, dishonored a century ago
we could have been throbbing inside each other now
inside this naked marble room, filled to the heights of
madness and burning down around us in streams.
we could have been the wasted expectation of millions and
the failure of ourselves. we could have been the heads of
state, the heads of spiders, the heads of kingdoms, the
heads of heretics beheaded, the 7 heads of a single myth.
we could have been caged, sold, knighted, baptized.
we could have been lovers behind each other's backs.
we could have been the rain that mocks the rainmaker,
the aches that stroke each other's release.
we could have been the ones you write about touching.
we could have been anyone we could have been.

// strong //

darkness broke free of the dawn
hours before us
watching the rain fall and the mist
of things held back rising up.
the desires of pine cone trees seem
altogether different when they stretch
instead from side to side
and reject the sky.
i'm the taste of feathered ink, white lace
candy and temporary satisfaction.
you hand me strong coffee
in a fragile cup
the day, the rain keeps falling,
i stay still and watch
as you get up.

// collection //

you'd love to arrange me
wouldn't it be perfect?
compliant as modeling clay wrapped in wet
plastic atop the platform you've only half
finished, nailed down in the hall
built to display collections of things
for not touching.
but i won't mind the sweat sliding inside the
thought wires we've locked around my wrists.
this is your doing - your undoing - now.
you always forget, my beautiful thief,
that i can count your steps from here
and time is nothing but sand
falling along the hour;
cascades of skin pulling away from
skin held still by the bend in the glass
and i'm not in this
for you.

// poetry //

upstairs
chipped fingers
work the hair away from the eyes.
i wake to
a sky that flashes too bright
beneath my open skin.
the bed, the sheets, the heat,
everything's too loud.

familiar, this.
these bones and i
will spend another day
together
wondering where all the good
poetry's
gone.

// endure //

even shadows mourn.
i can endure not touching so long.
as pages persist they write themselves
turning sheets upon sodden sheets into
wet leaves peeling each other.
rest is forbidden here.
the deliberate pattern repeats: back to
front
to back
to front
as fingers teasing, touching, kneading
the white of the ink my blood red
lips part and erase.
as the heavy soak of pewter clouds spreads
our thirst wider than the reach of rain, we
overtake one another, moving darkness
steady across three windows
and out to cover the globe. i submit and
endure. it only lasts so long.

// echo //

her voice has become my voice
severed and delivered back.
picture together both sides of the distance
that splits the face of a ghost in two
and tries to speak to you
from behind the glass.
echoes, courting each other's desire to be
heard, deny and satisfy each other.
one can never scream
without the other. the question answers the
question.
neither silence goes first.
when will you
LISTEN, goddamn it.
"when will
you."

// clocks //

again to me navigating the dim
unwelcome morning light,
a softness i could swear is killing me.
breathing fades to balancing on particles as they
catch my skin, part and spin
and fall
crawling into hairline fractures drawn
along porcelain faces - too many clocks
on the walls
inside you.
iron hands refuse the touching of each other
frozen like me
on the other side of my reflected eyes.
i'm always checking the time checking the time checking
the
time
checking the time and it's always the same always
[[[the same always the same]]]
we are warned of madness but time doesn't stop
just because glances do and i may be alone
but my mind still plays the game.

// fireplaces //

we tear at each other
hang bones over fireplaces.
we are the wounded, wounding.
we are the hunted, hunting.
we are the broken breaking
each other
down.
and here before me
is you.
the light we're fighting this darkness for
the one i'll take the wounds
without wounding
for
the one i'll swallow the hunt

and stop hunting for.
the one i fall broken before
praying for the strength to try not to
break anymore.

// fed //

turn me for now: sideways
and give to me your silence.
run like silken threads spun thick into ropes
inside me
inject it hot
down through my
veins
fast like wet city streets
in camera light
nothing to listen for any longer
finally nothing
to deafen the quiet
i'm made of and fed
on and fed to and bled for
seeping underneath
this costume i wear for them
that starves me only for you.
i'd like to take my silence now.
strip me clean of the words i've left.
let them watch close as you take them
without effort
easily
from
me.

// mask //

here: this is to hide the eyes.
now make me infinitesimal like
the pause between pauses in a
conversation you shouldn't hear
and stretched out quiet
wide
like a shadow but moving.
just allow yourself the inconvenient
pleasure of discovering me
as the mask of a face
inside your face
on the other side of the mirror
you're holding
face-down.
we're reflections of the same
reflection of silence:
only permissive
in the dark.

// ghost //

i'd not look quite like this if the fog
had not erased the fog.
imagine you in front of me
your fingers betray your mind
pressing smoke in impossible
attempts to trace my body
but i'm without skin so your fingers
are denied and only trace themselves.
would you like to try again?
i've been waiting centuries, beloved.
certain you'd remember
if this fog would just let up
and you could bear
to rid yourself
of fingers.

// touch //

i imagine him close
enough to hear his fingers
on my skin before the touch
he withholds too often.
far enough away,
the gold he touches
instead
turns cold
laid out across the floor.
the searing liquid once
made hot and poured
by imagining him close.

// thunder //

your voice is only static now
like the unwinding of
gears inside a felt lined box
inside a plastic girl
spinning.
we've never spoken
this way
and it's like sweating but tough to
maneuver
around the other things.
you're trying to remind me of memories
that are not ours
and my insides split open.
i search them for a reason to be on this connection

a way to get out of our punishing exchange
hissing and cracks mix heavy inbetween your voice
and the one i can't seem to find
but before i can move my mouth around "who's
there?"
a slam of thunder - close - disconnects the
line.

// face //

quiet like a stare
she stood in black rooms
by windows
watching for something more
permanent
than the fog
her wet breathing licked
inside the pane.
concentrating, trying
to recognize the faces
as they multiplied
and looked back in.

// grid //

you held my body to you
at odd angles
as if meeting my eyes
disrupted flight patterns
jamming calculated grids
across the sky
never connecting
but remarkably close by.

// ritual //

she pored over the words he left,
like her,
unattended.
poured them in a slanted line
along her wrists
bent back
like holy water
dragging
under a thousand bridges
setting
flesh on fire.
a ritual, a consecration, a way
to push up against the ghosts'
advancing.
words like tears.
rain for decades.

// manifesto //

if you're going to create
do it.
do it at the wrong time.
at odd hours.
publish too much and then
disappear.
don't follow
unfollow
the following

don't ever give the right answer.
if you are going to create
do it where it's cramped and
awkward.
who wants to write in the bright sun
in the wide sky?
i can't think like that.
the menacing space
the freedom
is too cruel
the light too upsetting.
if you are going to create
do it in the dark.
do it where the walls promise
to keep your mind safe from all the
running.